INCARNATION
Doctrine and Substance

Dr. George Bebawi

TRANSLATOR'S NOTE:

This is the English translation of a short Arabic book written by Dr. George Bebawi on the incarnation of our Lord Jesus Christ. The Arabic book is titled التجســـد، العقيدة والمضـــمون (*āltağsud*, *āl'qyda wāl-maḍmun)*, and is only one of many books that Bebawi has written in Arabic concerning the topic of the divine Incarnation.

A literal method has been adopted in translating, but without being too rigid. Words like شركة and اشتراك, which have multiple meanings in English, were difficult to translate; "communion," "partaking," "participation," and "sharing" were all utilized to translate such words to capture the true meaning the author is trying to convey. Other than these two, the remaining terms were consistently translated.

The Arabic text for this book does not utilize footnotes, but typically puts references within parenthesis. All parenthetical citations within the text are original to the author, any footnotes have been added by the translator for reference.

I pray that the reader may benefit from this work.

Translator
2023

TABLE OF CONTENTS

Roots of The Incarnation

St. Paul says, "God, who at various times and in various ways spoke in time past to the fathers by the prophets, has in these last days spoken to us by His Son, whom He has appointed heir of all things, through whom also He made the worlds" (Heb 1:1-2). Since ancient times, God has talked about Himself to the human and has revealed His secrets according to what would lead to a genuine human life.

In the Old Testament, the inspiration and appearances of God were not only manifestations of God alone, but also manifestations about the human also, because the human who sees and hears the Word of God shifts to a new relationship that God commands. The revelations and appearances transport the human from resistance and sin to obedience, holiness, and knowledge of God.

God has entered the human world with His superior ability to change life. This entrance takes place within the theme of the dominion of God over creation as their maker; for God does not enter the life of the creatures as an intruder, but as an owner, possessor, and giver of the gift of existence; "for in Him we live and move and have our being" (Acts 17:28).

Whenever God entered human life, He retained His divinity as a Creator. When he was made incarnate in the New Testament, salvation was described as a new creation in Jesus Christ. For God talks about Himself as a creator, maker, or artificer, which are the names given to God. God is a creator and maker because he brought everything out of non-existence. He is an artificer, for he formed and produced. This is a clear image that the human sees in the depth of life whenever one feels the presence of God and His creative ability, which cannot be comprehended by the human.

GOD: THE CREATOR AND SAVIOR

God has described himself several times as the Creator of the human and the maker of heavens and earth. However, we rarely notice that these divine discourses are all tied to one theme—the work of salvation. God's entrance into history, for the sake of the weak and sinful, is the picture that is clear in the prophets, and especially in Isaiah; worry reaches the human and his seed, for the human is subject to extinction by a fellow human.

The sharp and violent struggle causes human existence to be in danger. For the struggle is one of nations and kingdoms; it is then that God speaks. He stands as a just judge, judging all involved parties. It is rare in the Old Testament that one sees God involved for the benefit of one population against all others. That would be a partial and incomplete view; otherwise, how would one understand the prophet Jeremiah where he describes death, destruction, and desolation.

God is the just judge, who judges as the Psalm says, "Your arrows are sharp in the heart of the King's enemies; The peoples fall under You. Your throne, O God, is forever and ever; A scepter of righteousness is the scepter of Your kingdom" (Ps 45:5-6). The present discussion is not concerning a specific people, but rather about the battling humanity, in which a congregation wins; but at the end, God does not allow a human or people to be enslaved to another; this is the entire Old Testament.

However, why does God become involved as a judge? Because He is the Creator. There is a commitment for God towards His creation. Whatever has been given in the law is not enough for Him; instead, He holds the entire path of life. The Holy Bible, in both testaments, does not indicate a depiction of God who judges through the law only; for this is the picture of a human judge who enforces the law justly without feeling any belonging towards any of the defendants; this is not the true picture of God. It is true that He is the one who instituted the law, and is the first to abide by it; but at the same time, He is the Creator who sees the entire human life and knows that the law could not correct and enhance it. Instead, it is like the Apostle Paul says, the law was added because of Transgression.

Therefore, those who perceive God only as just in the Old Testament, and has changed His style to include mercy in the New Testament, offer a fractured judgement containing much inconsistency. Divine mercy occupies a special place in the Old Testament. It is the mercy of the Creator who takes its spiritual shape in the majority of the Old Testament books in the word "salvation." How could God be a savior and be just only, delaying mercy for a better age? It is a question we rarely consider because we have perceived an incorrect separation between the two Testaments. When God abides by the law, he abides by its entirety. He was exercising His role as a king, who possesses the destinies of all creatures; He was doing this as Savior and Judge at the same time. Here, judgement is not the separation in the case of wisdom; instead, judgement itself takes the shape of salvation at times, whenever God is involved to give support to the oppressed, doing so through the divine mercy that flows from Him as a creator. God has given the law to the human, but as Creator, He knows the truth of creation and was prepared for the transgression of the law, meaning that the law would not become the basis for eternal relationship with God. For God, who sees all the ages of the human, has planted and revealed eternity in the mortal earthly life. Eternity is not built on the law, regardless of its kind and success; instead, it is based on the life that springs from the Creator. Therefore, the role of the law was a temporary role, which the Apostle described as the role of the instructor or mentor until the coming of perfection, which is the new law of life in Christ.

GOD: THE EVER-PRESENT

The Old Testament, especially, is the book of the "Divine I am."
For God says, "I am the Lord." He says this to emphasize His
continual presence through communicating with humankind.
The divine word—which is the human image comprised of
letters and words—have transported the divine presence to the
human life. However, the Old Testament did not investigate the
efficacy of God speaking with the human, nor the problem of
God using a human language. Such research stems from
philosophical and logical problems, which has no existence in
God's relationship with the human, but it was invented by the
non-religious human who sees, in the experience of religion, a
number of human problems deriving from human need,
expressing human pain and wishes. From here, the religious
doctrine in contemporary philosophical schools became simply
human emotions and longings with no divine basis—God is
non-existent, the human alone is existent, and the experience of
atheism is what created the problem of the human language. The
connection between human language and faith has not been
studied except in the absence of God from human life or His
inability to speak human language. This problem only appears in
periods of spiritual weakness, prior to the Middle Ages.

The human of the Old Testament knew that God is able to
speak with him as Creator and did not see any problem in this.
For the Creator, who formed the first human out of dust, did

not hesitate to grant speech; He did so in order to hear the human, but also so that He could speak and the human would listen. In the Old Testament, the verbs "hear" and "listen" were not applied in a strict manner to the ear or the movement of the tongue in speech, but rather to understanding, reaching a meaning, and discovering the purpose. Those who hear the word of God are those who understood what God wants. We might be even closer to accuracy if we say that hearing equals willing, for hearing and will are one. In the life of the modern human, however, one has grown to hear much but understand little. This is what made the contemporary problem, separating the will from hearing or understanding.

The speech of God—who is always present and says on every occasion, "I am the Lord"—is a speech of significance. For when He says, "I am the Lord," He returns to:

1. The schedules which He has pre-appointed and given through His mercy.
2. The salvific works, in which God has intervened and made; for example, foretelling what will come in the future.

God has said in the beginning of the Mosaic Law, "I am the Lord your God, who brought you out of the land of Egypt, out of the house of bondage" (Ex 20:2). Here, the divine presence reveals the superior power of God to the human. God has struck the pagan gods of Egypt and destroyed them, meaning that He is present in history and reveals Himself in confronting false gods. This revelation takes a few forms:

1. The event
2. The prophetic word
3. The promises

Through the event, God tells about Himself, for events are much stronger than words. God is not easy words; God becomes completely silent and allows His power to work what words could not accomplish accurately. The silence of God is an invitation for the human to contemplate how God works much without manifesting Himself directly.

Here, it is possible to understand that an event surpassing works, many times becomes discourse as the words at the beginning of the ten commandments. God has brought out His people with power and a outstretched arm, "Therefore say to the children of Israel: 'I am the Lord; I will bring you out from under the burdens of the Egyptians, I will rescue you from their bondage, and I will redeem you with an outstretched arm and with great judgments" (Ex 6:6). God did not stop at this, but talked much about the event as an example of salvation that He is able to accomplish and about the salvation coming in the future.

The event and the word, for God, are one instrument. The human may discern between them in the mind, but it is a different matter for God. He is present in the events as the All-Governing, and the presence of God does not separate between word and event in everything revealed and concealed.

Beginning of The Incarnation

God has foretold His coming in the flesh by more than one method in the Old Testament, so that we may easily see in these clear forms the beginning revelation of the Incarnation.

1. The apparitions of God to Abraham, Moses, Isaiah, and others.
2. The divine inspiration, which the desire of God to talk with the human in the language of the human.
3. The presence of God in the historical event and the movement of these events to fulfill His end and purpose.

We are also able to see this topic in a different, yet clearer, form if we always remember that the divine apparitions, inspiration, and salvific works in history are nothing other than true and clear spiritual signs that

1. God is Creator and has commitment toward His creation.
2. Creation without God would die, which is the subject of divine grace. It is the thing keeping creatures alive, and there is no differentiation between grace and mercy. The human enjoys divine grace in a much deeper level as the one who receives the words of God and enters

into the covenant which God offers to the one created in His image—the divine gift that allowed the human to enjoy the rational relationship with God.

3. The standing covenant is not by the presence of God alone, but also by the promise. When God promises by Himself, He binds Himself by a grounded foundation that could not be changed in the face of historical changes.

Incarnation and The Divine Oath[1]

God swore by Himself when He promised Abraham with blessings. It may seem that using the word "swore" is not appropriate, and we should not picture God as people who swear. Instead, the relationship between the sworn oath and the divine presence is clear; God who is present is confirming that He is unchanging, and His mercy does not disappear because of human sins. Therefore, He swears without regretting nor relenting, even as He foreknows exactly what spiritual atrocity the human will reach.

It is clear from the sworn oath, God has taken an entry point for His superior presence in history to confirm the fulfillment of the promises in confronting the human who is weak-willed, narrow-minded, and frequently wavering between good and evil. The sworn oath is the beginning of a relationship built on covenant (testament), which the sworn oath gives an ability to remain and pluck out the human from wavering. Here, God resorts to this human method to confirm His commitment as He has revealed in promises. Thus, the sworn oath in its simple image, just like apparitions and inspiration, is the fundamental presence of God in the human life.

---

[1] See Lk 1:73 for example.

WHY THE INCARNATION?

THE FIRST STAGE

The question about the reasons for the incarnation first arose through the ancient heresies, which presented two completely opposite positions:

1. Rejection of the human incarnation altogether, which was the position of the heresies during the first three centuries. They believed in the divinity of the Son, but completely denied that He incarnated, since it is unfit for God to become human. Because the human body is evil, it would be impossible for a good God to choose the evil body as an instrument by which to reveal Himself.

2. Rejection of the divinity of the Son, meaning a clinging to His humanity and complete denial of His divinity, which was the position of Arianism as condemned universally in the Council of Nicaea in 325 AD.

THE SECOND STAGE

This occurred after the fourth century, as an extension to the first stage, exhibiting Eutychianism and Nestorianism, at the two opposite ends. When Nestorianism denied the union of the humanity with divinity, Eutychianism also denied the union, preaching the dissolution of humanity within the divinity.

Because of these heresies it was impossible for the church fathers not to look for reasons for the incarnation. The search started from the time of Clement of Alexandria and has continued continuously. However, we need to stop at the main points the fathers have set in the first five centuries, without going into too much detail:

FIRST: THE INCARNATION WAS NECESSARY AS GOD'S REVELATION OF HIMSELF BECAUSE OF WHAT AFFLICTED THE HUMAN.

If the doctrine of the incarnation has its roots in the Old Testament, it is clear that these roots could not grow and be fruitful except in the New Testament. The fruit of such roots is the incarnation as the final revelation of God. This revelation does not negate what precedes it from manifestations; instead, it interprets it and explains it as seen in the opening of Hebrews, which confirms that perfection was through the coming of the Son.

SECOND: INCARNATION WAS NECESSARY AS A DIVINE EVENT THAT IS BEYOND THE POWER OF WORDS

1. The incarnation confirmed that God genuinely loves the human. Out of His abundant love, He united with the humanity. The unity here means that God accepted the human forever. For in uniting His divinity with a humanity like ours, it means that it has become impossible to separate between God and human.

   This truth is expressed in the union, and it is truly the intention of the incarnation itself. The union is an image and level signifying a strong relationship that does not accept what sin has planted, such as fear and a rejection of God's grace. For the humility of God clashes with the arrogance of the human, which makes the human unable to accept the grace of God.

The Fathers of the fourth and fifth centuries have recorded many observations regarding the Arian and Nestorian heresies, as to attempts for the sin and death in us to reject the grace of God. The Fathers have agreed that human arrogance is what makes Arianism a defensive position for the honor of God, which does not allow incarnation. The fear of Nestorianism regarding the union is nothing other than fear from the awareness and depth that incarnation places on the conscience of the human, especially, since the incarnation requires a complete emptying of arrogance or guarding the ego.

2. The incarnation has announced the downfall of all human means in coming closer to God, such as the complex rituals and animal sacrifices. Origen the scholar and Augustine after him have commented that what came in the old law—sacrifices, ritual washings, and other procedures—was resting on a very important foundation that the human alone is incompetent to appear between the hands of God, and thus, the human relied on other created elements, such as animals, which were originally created for the service of the human and placed under the feet of humanity's dominion before the fall.

These creatures had become, to an extent, a mediator

between God and the human. It was an expression of the loss of dominion of the human over creation, but in a deeper sense, the sacrifices express the human's need for grace. Since the human did not possess the ability to come near God without the conditions that God has placed, the human was no longer in possession of a good relationship with the Creator.

Therefore, the incarnation has expressed the demise of every means that the human offers. For God came and was incarnate, which put the human in a position of thanksgiving and praise towards the one who humbled Himself and came. Here we must clearly see that the old methods, which expressed the human's need for grace, have lost their power. "For the law was given through Moses, but grace and truth came through Jesus Christ."[2] The expression in the Gospel of John, "of His fullness we have all received, and grace for grace,"[3] directly means that grace is 'The presence of the Son in the flesh.'

Interpreters have finally noticed a very important point in the prologue of the Gospel of John, the first to note it was the Scholar Origen. It is the relationship of the Logos with the creation. For all that is in creation came through the will of the Logos and all the rational creatures are enlightened by Him. He is the light without which there would be no light. However, the good news of the gospel is not that the Logos created all the creatures, but that He who is from the beginning came and was incarnate. Not shinning as a creator who is coming with life from the darkness of the abyss, but rather He comes with life to the light of the communion with the Father (Origen *Com Jo* 1.14).

---

[2] Jn 1:17.
[3] Jn 1:16.

For grace is not given to those who have and live, but to those who do not have and are in the grasp of death. Here we recognize the importance of the incarnation as a great event that changed the relationship between God and the human. For the human looks for refuge in the bosom of the Father where the mediator is, and He is the mediator of a better covenant, that is Jesus Christ.

We can understand the meaning of grace if we remember that the existence and life of the human depend on God, and God alone. There is no ability within the human nature itself to continue life and remain in existence. God alone is the essence of existence, but the creatures are subject to nonexistence and dissolution; the one who keeps them from non-existing is God.

   3.   The union of divinity with humanity has made perfectly clear the intentions of God:

       a.   The human will never perish since Christ will remain forever as an incarnate God.

       b.   The separation bet God and the human are completely removed and the goodness of the divinity could easily pass to the human, because the new head of humanity carries it in Himself and from Him to his brethren. He is the head and source from whom all divine blessings flow down to the members.

       c.   Divinity remained as is without any decrease; what increased is the humanity. It increased, meaning that it transformed from separation and isolation from God to unity without mixing, confusion, or alteration.

Here, the union along with all its previous terms relate to

Christ, but also relate to us in any discussion about grace. Our likeness to Christ does not offer an equality with Christ, for the difference between creation and incarnation is very massive. Incarnation is the coming of the Son, the second hypostasis of the Trinity, to unite with humanity. However, creation is the making of the human from nothing and it is a making that is based fundamentally on the human not existing in itself, but as the creation of a creator who does not receive His existence from another. Thus, the human remains unable to become like the Son. For the human is not a hypostasis in the Trinity, and hence we unite with the divinity without becoming ourselves divinity; our created essence does not change into the essence of the Creator, for this is what is meant by mixing and confusion.

If we remain as we are in the created nature, yet we become participants in the divine nature, "by which have been given to us exceedingly great and precious promises, that through these you may be partakers of the divine nature, having escaped the corruption that is in the world through lust" (2 Pt 1:4). This clearly assures that we will remain created as we are, because our partaking in the divine nature does not at all mean that we would lose our created being. Against such perversion, the patristic teaching stands against Eutychianism which called for the dissolution of the humanity within the divinity.

INCARNATION AND THE
TRUTH OF DIVINE GRACE

Since we take from His fullness, "of His fullness we have all received, and grace for grace,"[4] and He is the only Son, then we should not make distinction between humanity and divinity, except for distinction in thought only to be able to understand the incarnation as explained by St. Cyril of Alexandria. "Of His fullness we have all received, and grace for grace,"[5] It is clear that we can not divide the one Christ into two natures as the Syrian Fraction says, reflecting the understanding of both Cyril of Alexandria and Severus of Antioch.

This makes us stand at the meaning of divine gift. For we have received the life of Christ and this superior gift is not a gift that is from the created nature, since this was the Arian interpretation. Also, it is not a human gift, for this was the Nestorian interpretation, which made the body of Christ only a human body, granting nothing to those who receive it in the Mystical Supper. However, if we receive Christ, truly and really, then we surely cannot see grace as anything other than the direct presence of God and His divine work in us, which cannot be separated from His hypostasis. In his third letter to Nestorius, St. Cyril confirms the truth of the incarnation:

---

[4] Jn 1:16.
[5] Jn 1:16.

Neither do we say that the Word of God dwelled, as in an ordinary man, in the one born of the Holy Virgin, in order that Christ might not be thought to be a man bearing God. For even if the Word both "dwelt among us," and it is said that in Christ "dwells all the fullness of the Godhead bodily," we do not think that, being made flesh, the Word is said to dwell in him just as in those who are holy, and we do not define the indwelling in him to be the same. But united *kata phusin*, and not changed into flesh, the Word produced an indwelling such as the soul of man might be said to have in its own body.[6]

Here, we could see that any distortion in the understanding of the incarnation translated to a distortion in the understanding of grace. For Christ is not like other saints (those who are holy), as made clear by the text. Christ is God who dwelt in humanity just like the union of the soul with the body in the human. St. Cyril confirms in the same letter, "Therefore Christ is one, both Son and Lord not by reason of a man having simply a conjoining to God."[7] This is an essential difference between the human and Christ.

St. Cyril then says,

Neither indeed do we think that the manner of the 'conjoining' is according to a juxtaposition', for this is not sufficient for a personal union, nor indeed according to a nonessential participation, as we also, who cleave to the Lord

---

[6] Third Letter to Nestorius, 9. English translation taken from: *St. Cyril of Alexandria: Letters*, trans. John I. McEnerney (Washington, DC: Catholic University of America Press, 2007), 83-84.
[7] Third Letter to Nestorius, 10.

according to the Scripture, are one spirit with him, but rather we reject the term 'conjoining' as not being sufficient to signify the union.[8]

The source of personality in the incarnate one is the Logos, and this is why St. Cyril rejects any depiction of words about the union, except a true union. St. Cyril then reaches the intention of speaking about the union, saying,

> Proclaiming the death according to the flesh of the only begotten Son of God, that is, of Jesus Christ, and confessing his Resurrection from the dead and his Ascension into heaven, we celebrate the unbloody sacrifice in the churches, and we thus approach the spiritual blessings and are made holy, becoming partakers of the holy flesh and of the precious blood of Christ, the Savior of us all. And we do this, not as men receiving common flesh, far from it, nor truly the flesh of a man sanctified and conjoined to the Word according to a unity of dignity, or as one having had a divine indwelling, but as the truly life-giving and very own flesh of the Word himself. For, being life according to nature as God, when he was made one with his own flesh, He proclaimed it life-giving. Wherefore even if he may say to us, "Amen, I say to you: Except you eat the flesh of the Son of Man, and drink his blood," we shall not conclude that his flesh is of someone as of a man who is one of us, (for how will the flesh of a man be life-giving according to its own nature?)[9]

For this reason, the fathers used a very important Greek term regarding the nature of the work of grace, which is the term *Theandric Acts*. The fathers describe the soul of Christ as human

---

[8] Third Letter to Nestorius, 10.
[9] Third Letter to Nestorius, 12.

with "divinely human" breaths (Gregory of Nyssa, Homily 3:8 on John). All the works of Christ were not human nor divine, but "divinely human" (Dionysius the Areopagite letter 4).

The grace is a divine gift, which is the life of Christ that is undivided between God and human. This is what is understood from *Theandric*, which is made of two parts *The-* meaning divine and *-andric* meaning human. This word was popularized in the Eastern Non-Caledonian church, especially in the time of Philoxenus of Mabbug and Severus of Antioch for describing Christ in an orthodox manner to avoid dividing Him into two— one son of God, and the other son of man.

From here we can see all the attempts in analyzing the divine grace which the Father bestowed upon us through His Son, Jesus Christ. We must adhere to the apostolic tradition, otherwise, we would fall into Arianism or the denial of Nestorianism. The difference between the apostolic faith and that of Arianism or Nestorianism is:

1. Grace is a direct work of the hypostasis of the incarnate God.

2. It is an uncreated gift and should not be credited back to the created natures, for this would mean that the Son, the second hypostasis, did not incarnate.

3. It is partaking of the Divine nature. For denying this participation means that human nature would not receive the goodness of the divinity, which would ultimately lead, not only to deny the incarnation of the God's Son, but also to consider the human not in need of the grace of eternal life coming from God.

INCARNATION AND THE
SUBSTANCE OF GRACE

St. John says that "the Word became flesh and dwelt in us." This phrase, along with others, especially those famous ones of St. Paul the Apostle where he uses prepositions such as "in" or "of" or "from" all especially point out that divine grace is "a direct presence of the Trinity: the Father, Son, and Holy Spirit." This presence reaches its clear shape in the beginning of Christian life as we are baptized in Christ, "For as many of you as were baptized into Christ have put on Christ" (Gal 3:27). This is what makes all the baptized to be one in Christ, since "there is neither Jew nor Greek, there is neither slave nor free, there is neither male nor female; for you are all one in Christ Jesus" (Gal 3:28).

Thus, we can see that baptism is an entrance into participation in God in Jesus Christ and by the Holy Spirit. This entrance cannot be accomplished without the incarnation. The basic power of baptism is in the mediation of Christ, which St. Paul expresses powerfully in Romans 6:

We are united with Him in the likeness of His death (Rom 6:5)	We are buried with Him in baptism (Rom 6:4)
The old man has been crucified with Him (Rom 6:6)	We become alive by His resurrection (Rom 6:5)
We will live again with Him (Rom 6:8)	We died with Him (Rom 6:8)
	Alive to God in Christ Jesus our Lord (Rom 6:11)

It is clear that a picture cannot be given to grace other than the substance of direct participation in the divine life that God has bestowed upon us in His Son Jesus Christ. This is the clear truth behind the words of the Apostle John, noting the difference in words only.

The Word become flesh, dwelt among us, and we saw His glory (Jn 1:14)
The Only-Begotten of the Father, full of grace and truth (Jn 1:14)
From His fullness we have all taken (Jn 1:16)
Grace above grace (Jn 1:16)

We are born of God directly. This birth would be impossible without the incarnation because the incarnation is the only shared element between us and the Only Son, which made Him "the firstborn among many brethren" (Rom 8:29). Hence, we are able to participate in the grace of Christ, which is His life that He pours within us through the Holy Spirit: "For you did not receive the spirit of bondage again to fear, but you received the Spirit of adoption by whom we cry out, 'Abba, Father.' The Spirit Himself bears witness with our spirit that we are children of God" (Rom 8:15-16).

This grace is the participation in God, and it does not mean at all that we can gain anything else other than Christ Himself. That is the meaning of the verse "and if children, then heirs—heirs of God and joint heirs with Christ, if indeed we suffer with Him, that we may also be glorified together" (Rom 8:17). Here we must understand that we change to the image of the incarnate God, and not the image of God in an unbounded way. Hence the shared element is the humanity, not the divinity. Therefore, the image of our glorious life is the humanity. We are all sharers in the body as the Apostle Paul says, "that the Gentiles should be fellow heirs, of the same body, and partakers of His promise in Christ through the gospel" (Eph 3:6). However, this sharing is not done without the divinity. Here we must remember the monumental lesson we learned from Nestorianism, which is that we cannot separate the humanity and divinity in the one Christ. Thus, our communion is not with the humanity of Christ without His divinity. For the Lord Jesus Himself said, "It is the Spirit who gives life; the flesh profits nothing. The words that I speak to you are spirit, and they are life" (Jn 6:63).

From this angle, we must realize that if we take the humanity of Christ without His divinity, then we are denying the incarnation. Discussing the incarnation would not be fitting at all except if we recognize that the Son truly incarnated and became flesh. However, we must go back to what we have said previously that we transform into the image of glorified Christ, but it is not the image of Christ before the incarnation but after. What carries into the communion with the divinity is the humanity.

Here, it appears clearly what Christ revealed for us is our life which has become glorified in Him. This life is our life as we have seen it—His incarnation, death, resurrection, ascension, and sitting at the right of the Father. "When Christ who is our life appears, then you also will appear with Him in glory" (Col 3:4).

The discussion here is regarding human life, which has been glorified because of divinity, becoming one with His divinity without mixing, confusion, or alteration. This, in turn, explains for us that "we all, with unveiled face, beholding as in a mirror the glory of the Lord, are being transformed into the same image from glory to glory, just as by the Spirit of the Lord" (2 Cor 3:18). This very image is not the image of the divinity without humanity nor the image of the humanity without divinity, but the image of the one Christ.

INCARNATION AND PARTICIPATION IN THE HYPOSTATIC ATTRIBUTE

The dogma of the universal church is that the Trinity is one essence and three hypostases. Each hypostasis is distinguished from the other by a hypostatic attribute—Fatherhood, Sonship, Proceeding. Fatherhood is special to the Father alone, and it is what makes the first hypostasis Father. Likewise, the Sonship and the Proceeding, which is called at times the giving.

The incarnation has made it for us a reality to share in the Son's hypostatic attribute, which is the Sonship. This attribute is not exclusive to the body or the humanity at all, for the body or humanity that is taken from the virgin is a participant in our nature, which is not at all associated with divinity. It was a human body like our body, but when the Son of God dwelt in the body, He made it humanity, or the body, His own special body and because of the union, the body became inseparable from Him— God the Son. This is the meaning behind what St. Paul says, "But when the fullness of the time had come, God sent forth His Son, born of a woman, born under the law, to redeem those who were under the law, that we might receive the adoption as sons" (Gal 4:4-5).

HOW DID ADOPTION
REACH US?

Not through the humanity—this is what made Nestorianism
very dangerous for salvation—but through the divinity.
However, we have no communion with the divinity. The
Sonship of the Son to the Father is the communion with the
Father, Son, and Holy Spirit. It does not proceed at all from the
created natures. However, how can we participate in this
superior sonship if we are children of the flesh, born according
to the limited law of nature, which could not give the human the
ability to receive something exclusive to God that is above all
creation?

St. John the Evangelist says that this is the gift of God that
all those who accept Him, He has given to them to become
children of God, to those who believe in His name: who were
born, not of blood (created nature), nor of the will of the flesh
(human ability), nor of the will of man (fruit of marriage or
natural law) (cf. Jn 1:12-13). Here, it becomes clear to us the
meaning of the union of the divinity with humanity in the one
Christ, and the meaning of the patristic struggle against
Nestorianism. The sonship that we take is the authority of God,
which we receive by faith. It is an authority that surpasses the
comprehension of all people, above all capacities, abilities, and
intentions of all created natures.

We cannot call our sonship to God anything other than participation in the hypostatic attribute of the Son; He makes us sons to God. Like the Holy Spirit proceeds from the Father and rests in the Son, He also rests in us as children of God in Christ, and allows us to say like Christ "Abba, Father."

Words do not allow to speak of participation hypostatic attribute of the Father and the hypostatic attribute of the Holy Spirit, which is sanctification—the name for the superior gift which makes us temples of God through the Holy Spirit. However, an important question remains: does our participation in the sonship of the Son make us children of the Father exactly like the Son? In answering this question, we must admit that it is an incorrect question for several reasons:

1. It ignores that the Son is the Only Son, who has no other with Him. It also ignores that in the incarnation the Only Son came down to be human; for the source of the personality is the Logos for the Son, whereas the source of the personality within us is the created human will.

2. The human is not incarnated, but created. The body is the self-nature and there is no uncreated nature in it such as divinity; it would be impossible.

3. Participation in the Sonship of the Son is a grace that comes externally, as St. Athanasius has emphasized. This means that such grace is not a nature within us, but a grant that is not at all associated with the created nature. This means that grace is always connected to the will of the giver, thus God has not granted us to transform into the essence of divinity. The will of the Father has been revealed to us in the grace of adoption

with us remaining as brethren to the first fruit—The Only Son. Hence, grace works within us according to the divine intention, meaning that we remain human as we are. This is especially apparent in the Resurrection of Christ and entrance of His humanity into the eternal glory to remain without perishing, being absorbed, or dissolution. Because of the union, we too do not dissolve but receive glory.

4. The question regarding the kind of glory and essence of grace has no place at all, as long as we believe in the unity of the one Christ. For the divine glory shined from Christ in a visible way on the mountain of the Transfiguration, which was a glory that is latent within Him; Christ did not uncover it from another, but it is the glory of His own self.

Here we must understand the intention of the glorious manifestation on the mountain. We do not become like Christ, shining in us a self-glory from within; instead, it is the divine glory that shines from without and is reflected upon us. It is one of the fruits of our union with Christ; thus, if we lost our union, we lost everything.

Christ is the one who shines in us, and this means that we have been transformed to His glory by the grace coming to us without us ourselves becoming the source of glory, but we have been glorified with Him because we share in Him. If the human would become absolutely like God in everything, this would mean the cessation of communion between God and the human.

The gifts of God are self-based because He is the initiator of existence. However, what the human receives is a gift and grant; therefore, the existence of the human itself depends on divine grace. The union of divinity with the humanity was the intention of the coming of the Son of God in the body along with His death, resurrection, and ascension. Without the union, the incarnation would lose its meaning and the cross and resurrection would become of no value at all.

Made in the USA
Middletown, DE
24 September 2023

39260453R00026